Ask COSMO *girl!*

About Guys

**All the Answers to Your Most Asked
Questions About Love and Relationships**

Ask COSMOgirl!

About Guys

All the Answers to Your Most Asked
Questions About Love and Relationships

From The Editors of CosmoGIRL!

Hearst Books
A Division of Sterling Publishing Co., Inc.
New York

Library of Congress Cataloging-in-Publication Data
Ask CosmoGirl! about guys : all the answers to your most asked questions about love and relationships / from the editors of CosmoGirl.
    p. cm.
  Includes bibliographical references and index.
  ISBN 1-58816-485-3 (alk. paper)
  1. Dating (Social customs)—Miscellanea. 2. Interpersonal relations in adolescence—Miscellanea. 3. Teenage girls—Psychology—Miscellanea. 4. Teenage boys—Miscellanea. 5. Questions and answers. I. Title: Ask Cosmo girl! about guys. II. Cosmo girl.
  HQ801.A822 2006
  306.73'0835—dc22

                           2005013109

10 9 8 7 6 5 4 3 2 1

Book design by Margaret Rubiano

CosmoGIRL! is a registered trademark of Hearst Communications, Inc.

www.cosmogirl.com

For information about custom editions, special sales, premium and corporate purchases, please contact Sterling Special Sales Department at 800-805-5489 or specialsales@sterlingpub.com.

Distributed in Canada by Sterling Publishing
c/o Canadian Manda Group, 165 Dufferin Street
Toronto, Ontario, Canada M6K 3H6

Distributed in Australia by Capricorn Link (Australia) Pty. Ltd.
P.O. Box 704, Windsor, NSW 2756 Australia

Printed in China

Sterling ISBN 13: 978-1-58816-485-8
ISBN 10: 1-58816-485-3

Photo credits: Christy Bush, pg. 108; Saye, pg. 10, 28, 42, 72, 82, 90, 100; Martynka Wawrzyniak, pg. 58.

CoNTEnTs

FoReWoRd

From Me to You

CosmoGIRL!s love guys. Not only are they cute, they're also really great to be around. They have this way of looking for fun in everyday things and just living in the moment, which, let's face it, a lot of us girls don't always remember to do. And did you ever notice that sometimes guys have just the right outside perspective on a situation and that they can give really good advice? Plus, they can just be so sweet! They know just the right thing to say or do to make your day. That's the good stuff. That's why we keep 'em around! But because they also do things that are frustrating, annoying, confusing, or all of the above, we get hundreds of e-mails from you with your boy questions. How do I know if he likes me? Why is he cool to me one minute and he ignores me the next? Do you think I should make a move and ask him out? Those three questions are definitely in the top ten guy dilemmas you come to us with and that we answer in various ways in the magazine each month. But, we thought, why not put all the answers together for you in one book? That way, no matter what your situation—you've got a crush on a guy, you're going out with a guy, you just broke up with a guy, whatever—you've got the information you need to navigate your love life, all in one place. Because one thing's for sure about guys; as soon as you think you have 'em figured out, they throw you another curve ball! Anyway, I hope this book is helpful to you now and for years to come. But just remember one thing: even though it sometimes seems like it, guys are not the enemy! They're just programmed differently, and we just have to accept that it often takes a little more effort to understand them. But once you do make that effort, you're one step closer to being able to enjoy all the funny and sweet and cool things—all the good stuff—about those mysterious beings called boys!Feel free to keep your questions coming to me, CG!s. I'm here for you at susan@cosmogirl.com. See you in the magazine!

Love,

ChApTeR 1

get that guy!

Whether you have your eye on a special someone or you're just boy crazy at the moment, you're not alone . . . everyone has been in a similar predicament. Read on for the best advice we've given to CosmoGIRL!s in situations like yours, involving everything from how to approach your crush, how to talk to that special guy, and more!

GeT ThAt GuY!

Q "I've always had trouble getting the really hot guys to talk to me. It seems like they're only interested in the gorgeous girls. I have a great personality, I'm fun to be with, and I have a good sense of humor. How do I get a great guy to be interested in me?"

A We believe there's someone for everyone "A cover for every pot," as they say. So if you want to get a great guy to be interested in you, be yourself and know that someone will love you for your personality—just the way you are. Unfortunately, you can't *make* anyone be interested in you, so don't even waste your time and energy trying! You can, however, look your best, smile, and put yourself in the right social situations to meet that right guy (chances are, *he'll* be into some of the same things you are). After that, sorry to say, it's out of any girl's control. Good luck!

Q "There's this one guy in my chemistry class who's really cute and I always try and partner up with him, but he always picks someone else. I've even offered to do his homework for him if he worked with me, but he always says no. What am I doing wrong?"

A Want to know what you're doing wrong? Okay, here goes. First if you do his homework for him, then what—his laundry? Trying too hard actually drives guys away. Believe it or not, guys like a little challenge when it comes to getting girls. So stop fixating on them, and instead, throw yourself into hobbies you're passionate about. You'll be too busy to worry about having a boyfriend. And that's usually when you meet the right guys anyway.

GeT ThAt GuY!

Q "I'd like to have a boyfriend, but I don't like anyone specifically. The junior prom is coming up, and my friends are worried that I won't have a date because I'm not going after anyone right now. But if I don't have a date, couldn't I just go with the group? Do I really have to have a date just because all my friends do?"

A Actually, you don't. And guess what? The fact that you're so comfortable about the idea of going to the prom alone if that's what ends up happening can actually work in your favor. It shows a lot of confidence and independence, which guys find really sexy. And because you're not dying for guys' attention, these strong qualities of yours are what will actually end up attracting guys to you—all the time. Pretty cool, huh?

CG! TIP: Be approachable. When you're friendly to everyone, that's the best way to meet others—especially guys!

Q "I like this guy, but I've never been that good at talking to guys—forget about letting them know how I feel about them! I like him so much that when I pass him in the hall, I can't even look at him because I'm afraid he'll see my feelings written all over my face. Every time I see him, I can feel my face turning bright red—and I don't want him to see that. I'd really like to date him. How can I let him know that I'm interested in him without totally embarrassing myself?"

A And guess what? Guys can't read your mind to know you like them, so they need some encouragement from you. This guy could even be interpreting your shyness as indifference, which you know isn't the case! So try to overcome your fears by making baby steps, even if it's just making eye contact at first. When you see him in the hall, hold your head high, keep your shoulders back, take a deep breath and nod a little hello when you pass him—and don't forget to smile! Eventually, you'll build up confidence, which is the sexiest flirting tool of all. And before you know it, you'll be saying hello to him, and working your way up to a full conversation. If you ask him about himself, he'll catch on that you like him soon enough—but you have to help him out a little bit. Remember: the key here is baby steps!

GeT ThAt GuY!

Q "Now that summer's here, my friends and I are looking to meet new guys. Any suggestions?"

A If you want to meet new guys, take charge of your summer social schedule and be the one who creates the fun. Host weekly backyard barbeques with friends—and have them host some too. Invite everyone you know and tell them to bring their friends. Without even trying, you'll come into contact with guys you might never have met otherwise. Once everyone knows that it's a regular thing where they'll meet new people, the crowd will grow. Plus, whenever you come across a new guy you want to see again, you instantly have a no-pressure way to ask him out—just mention that you're having a few friends over on a Thursday and tell him he should stop by. It's perfect: Lots of guys, zero maintenance, and fun with your friends. Get ready for an awesome summer!

Q "Most of my friends like just one guy, but I can't help myself: I like them all! Okay, well maybe not all of them...but a lot of them. My friends tell me I flirt too much, but I love the attention I get from the guys I flirt with. Is there something wrong with that?"

A If you're looking to get a reputation as the class flirt, then we guess there's nothing wrong with that. But if you're eventually looking to be with just one guy, you've got to slow down! It's okay to have crushes on a few different guys, but you can't date everyone! Trying to attract every guy you meet might give you a self-esteem charge, but what if a guy you just like to flirt with, who you're not that interested in, actually likes you a lot? Leading him on by flirting with him all the time could hurt his feelings—and you don't want to earn that kind of rep. Our advice? Seek out other confidence-boosters (like hobbies) and flirt more selectively. That way, you'll leave yourself open to having a healthy one-on-one relationship when you're ready for it.

GeT ThAt GuY!

Q "I'd like to have a boyfriend, but I'm busy all the time. Between studying for my advanced classes, keeping up with my column for the school paper, and my part-time job, not to mention hanging out with my friends, I barely have time to do all my homework and get enough sleep. Will I ever have a boyfriend?"

A Don't get mad at us for saying this, but you might not actually be "girlfriend material" right now. You feel secure in yourself, and your friends and interests fill up most of your time. You don't *need* a guy to make you feel special. The other side of that is that you have so many things going on that you don't have time for love. That's great, as long as you're not making yourself busy all the time because you're scared about getting close to someone. But you sound like you're happy and just haven't found someone who you feel as passionate about as you do the other things in your life. Don't worry, the right guy will come along. Just remember: the kind of person who will make you happiest when you're ready will probably be someone who appreciates all of your passions and has similar interests to yours.

Q "I want to fall in love more than anything else in the world. If I could make any wish come true, it would be that. I'm so desperate to make it happen, but it seems like it never will. What should I do?"

A The best way to fall in love? Stop looking for it! Right now, you may be sending vibes out into the universe that you're lonely, and that kind of energy can only attract more loneliness, not love. Ever notice that when you're happy, everyone is nicer to you? It's the same with love. Imagine the perfect guy in your life. Then think of things that are blocking you from being with him—a friend who makes you feel unpretty, a crush who has a girlfriend, and so on. Being aware of the blocks keeping you from finding love is the first step to removing them. Clear your path to love, and soon you'll find it sooner than you think.

GeT ThAt GuY!

Q "There's this guy I like who I really want to be with. We're so much alike: Both at the top of our class and also very social. The problem is, we're both really competitive and end up fighting with each other a lot. I know we can be this great power couple if only we could get along. What can I do to make it happen for us?"

A You may just want to rethink whether you want to get involved with another *you*. Think about it. In your life, amazing opportunities have always come to you because you rarely back away from what you want—and that's awesome, CosmoGIRL! But that doesn't mean all guys are right for your strong personality. You may want to be with another go-getter, which is what this guy sounds like to us, but just because you are alike in so many ways doesn't mean you're *compatible*. When two strong personalities come together, more often than not, they clash, just like with this guy. As you already have realized, there's a lot of competition for that spotlight, and only one of you can really have it at a time. So who would work better for you? Believe it or not, a shyer guy might be your best bet—he'll appreciate your take-charge attitude and that fact that you can say exactly what you mean. Instead of clashing with each other, like you do with this guy you like, you'll actually be able to balance each other out!

Q "I feel like I'm really ready to have a relationship. I know exactly what kind of guy I'm looking for. There are a lot of artsy guys and jocks in my school—but I'm not interested in that type. My ideal guy is more of a high-tech brainy guy— and he has to be really, really cute. So where can I find him?"

A If you're really serious about having a great relationship with someone who's really right for you, the best thing you can do for yourself is to set aside preconceived ideas of what you want in a guy. That mentality will just get in the way of your meeting new people. Consider every guy to be on a level playing field—they all have potential. Maybe artsy guys or athletes aren't usually your thing. But don't dismiss them before you find out what's beneath the surface. Hey—what if you learned that Mr. Artsy did the CD cover art for Limp Bizkit? Maybe the jock has a soft spot for the poetry of Rilke. Or that either of them are really computer savvy and smart? You'll never know unless you take the time to get to know them. Think of it this way: What if he wrote *you* off because he doesn't like girls with your hair color? Look what he'd be missing out on!

CG! TIP: If you can make him laugh, a light goes on in his head. He thinks, "Hey, this girl is really fun!" And he'll want to get to know you better.

GeT ThAt GuY!

Q "I just got out of a serious relation-ship, and instead of getting involved with just one person, I'd like to date a lot of guys right now and see how it goes. Does that make me a slut?"

A Not necessarily, but there are some guidelines you need to follow if you're going to be dating "buffet style" for now. For one, you have to let any guy you're involved with know the deal. Just because you're playing the field doesn't mean the guys you're dating are too. Some of them might be looking for something serious, or something seriously physical—which will defeat your purpose of casual dating. Set your own game rules and stick to them. For instance, you can flirt, but you can't make out with him one night and spend the next day having coffee with another guy. Guys have feelings too. So stick to the plan, keep the conversation light and skip the kiss good-night. That way, you can date the way you want to date without sending any mixed signals that might come back to haunt you *and* your reputation!

CG! TIP: Want to see if he's interested? Use the eye contact test. Make eye contact, then look away and look back. If he's still looking at you, go forth and conquer CosmoGIRL!

Q "I really like this guy at my school, but I have no idea how to approach him. He's always the center of attention because he's really funny. I think we could get along really well, as my friends always laugh at my jokes. But when it comes to cracking up guys, I just choke. What should I do?"

A We've all heard that the best way to steal a guy's heart is to make him laugh. But how can you get close enough to him to make him laugh without tripping all over yourself trying? Here's our advice. First, when you're using humor, always be positive. Laugh at life, not at your flaws. Putting yourself down makes you seem insecure or like you're fishing for compliments. You can tease him, but be sure to be playful about it—and remember to only tease him about things you like about him. Don't take it too far or you could hurt him. If you think he might take your joking the wrong way, don't risk it! Try to be spontaneous, even though it can be difficult when your heart is thumping around in your throat. Take something he says and work off it to make a joke. It shows you can think fast, be goofy, and really listen to what he has to say. He'll love it! Finally, stay in your comfort zone. If something feels weird to say—like a sex joke—don't say it. And who knows, soon you two might be sharing laughs together.

CG! TIP: Showing your sense of humor proves that you're confident—and that's sexy!

GeT ThAt GuY!

Q "There's this guy I know who's so cute, any girl would be so lucky to be his girlfriend! How can I get him to see that I'm worthy of being with him?"

A We have to be honest with you: you're a little turned around here. It should be about believing *the guy* would be lucky to be *your* boyfriend, and not the other way around. The secret is to be happy with yourself. Cliché? Maybe. But clichés are overused for a reason: they're true. Sharing your thoughts and your opinions with him will prove that you're confident. If you just tell a guy what he wants to hear, he'll get bored easily. So speak up and be his muse instead!

Q "I really like this guy, but he seems kind of insecure. I think he's really cute, but there are some things he doesn't like about himself, and he's always worried about them. How can I let him know that I think he's great just as he is?

A While it isn't your job to fix anyone, we all have our little insecurities that creep up on us and make us feel that we're not good enough. Why should guys be any different? That said, you don't need to give this guy a makeover or serious therapy, what you need is to casually give him little hints that he's great, and that those little flaws that he's so insecure about actually make him cuter and more interesting to you—not less. (Oh, and we're not saying to overlook a big flaw like an anger management problem or anything!) Your roll-with-it attitude will let him know he doesn't have to be self-conscious around you.

CG! TIP: If you're feeling sneaky, pretend you lost your cell phone and ask him to borrow his to call yours. That way, he'll have your number without you having to officially give it to him!

GeT ThAt GuY!

Q "I'd love to have a serious relationship with a guy. I want to experience romance and everything that goes along with it. But I don't want to be with just any guy, I want to be with the right guy. Does that make me crazy or something?"

A No, not at all. That you want to find someone to love is wonderful, but that you won't settle either is smart! How do you know if a guy is right for you? First of all, he should make your life enjoyable, not miserable. You have a great time with your friends, and you should expect nothing less than that from your relationship. If you're not happy when you're with him, that's a sign you should move on. The expression that "boyfriends are friends with benefits" is totally true. But in the rush to enjoy all the benefits of romance, it's easy to forget how important the friendship part is. It's not always about the kissing—it's about finding someone who wants to *help* put the finishing touches on your college essay or listen to you vent about a fight with your mom. It's only when you have that solid foundation that you can really experience all the best parts of being in love. But remember: As important as he is to you, you still need to find time for those things that make you who *you* are—and not just who you are as a couple.

Q "I really like this guy and I always try to say whatever I think he wants me to, but I still can't get him to like me. What's up with that?"

A You may not be giving him the chance to get to know you because you've been telling him everything you *think* he wants to hear. Now is the time to let him get to know you! How? When he asks you what you think of something, don't say "I don't know—what do you think?" Share your opinions with him. What's the worst that can happen? He won't agree with you. But that can actually be a good thing, because disagreements can lead to a discussion where you both voice your thoughts and learn things about each other. As long as you can always share your opinions, you'll always be discovering new sides of each other, and neither of you will get bored. So go ahead, express yourself!

ChAPTeR 2

a perfect romance

You've finally landed a great guy—yes, you have a boyfriend! How can you make the magic last? Check out the questions other CosmoGIRL!s have asked— and the advice we've given. Then apply it to your own guy situation.

A PeRfEcT RoMaNcE

Q "I want to get closer to my boyfriend, but he seems really closed off. How can I get him to open up to me?"

A Sometimes it really seems like guys keep their feelings locked up tighter than Fort Knox, but we have a few keys for opening their emotional vaults. First, be trustworthy. You wouldn't feel comfortable spilling to a gossip, right? So why would he? Don't dish dirt to him—why would he want to open up to you then? You might try sharing with him first. Tell him a personal story. It'll help foster a bond, and he'll more than likely follow your lead. If he feels like you trust him, he may feel more comfortable trusting you. When he does talk to you, be sure to listen carefully to what he says. Pay attention to him. Look into his eyes and be interested. Take his cue if he'd like your help or he just wants you to lend an ear. Whatever you do, don't force him to talk. If you pester him to open up, he may feel like you're treating him like his mom—and one mom is enough for anyone!

CG! TIP: To avoid TMI, take the time to get to know a guy and build up your trust before telling him too much about yourself.

Q "I wish my boyfriend would understand me without me having to explain myself to him all the time. I mean, sometimes I'm in a bad mood and I don't feel like talking and all he does is pester me with trivial things to try and make me talk to him. We've been together now for almost a year. Shouldn't he just know when something's wrong with me?"

A Hoping a guy will "just know" anything is a dream that rarely comes true. In fact, hoping anyone will just know anything about you is pretty unrealistic. There aren't many mind readers walking around out there! So, instead of getting on his case because he doesn't have John Edward's psychic abilities, why not talk to him about it? If you give a guy a chance to get it right by telling him what's going on right from the beginning of your relationship, eventually he'll start to see your patterns and read your signals. And by talking it through with him, you'll actually be improving your relationship. After all, the key to any great relationship is open communication.

CG! TIP: When it comes to past guy history, your new guy doesn't want to know *all* the details. Trust us!

A PeRfEcT RoMaNcE

Q "I've been going out with this guy for about three months and he's always so nice to me. He takes me to dinner, buys me presents, and sometimes leaves flowers in my locker. My mother warned me to look out for guys who are too nice—that they may just be setting me up to push me into having sex or something like that. But he has never even come close to that. I've told him I'm not ready and he said that was fine and he keeps doing nice things for me. Should I be waiting for the other shoe to drop?"

A It's easy to be skeptical, but you can't let the fear of what you believe may be true cloud up what's actually going on here. Now we don't know either of you at all, but from what you tell us, it sounds like this guy worships the ground you walk on—and in a very real way. He's not just kissing up to you because he wants something from you—he truly digs you. If this is the treatment you want him to keep up, and really, it should be, make sure you don't start taking how much he does for you for granted—always thank him for his thoughtful ways. Let him know how lucky you feel to have him in your life and how wonderful it is that he treats you so well. You may not always be able to reciprocate his adoring acts, but you can always let him know how much you appreciate them. He's not acting this way waiting for payback—he's acting this way because he really cares about you!

Q "I was looking for some original date ideas for me and my boyfriend. Got any suggestions?"

A There are lots of things you can do without resorting to the standard dinner-and-a-movie combo. You could go ice skating together or if there's a strong breeze outside, try flying a kite. That way, any time either of you sees a kite in the sky from that point on, whether you're together or not, you'll be thinking of each other. Have cars? Why not make a day of washing them together? Park both your cars in one of your driveways. Then get sponges, rags, soap, and a hose—and scrub away! See who can do the best job the fastest. (Throwing wet rags at each other is allowed!) After all, a little competition can be a very flirty thing! Now here's a really healthy suggestion: Make a plan to exercise together. Set aside a regular time for an active habit—tennis, jogging, whatever—that's just for you two. Being partners with a routine now will make him want to come back for your company—and the extra push to work out—later.

CG! TIP: Want to put a new spin on the traditional dinner date? Why not stay in and cook together one night? It's fun—and cheaper, too!

A PeRfEcT RoMaNcE

Q "I am so in love with my boyfriend. I think about him day and night and am miserable when we're not together or at least on the phone. I wish I could spend every minute with him. Is there anything wrong with that?"

A Wishing you can spend every minute together and actually doing so are two very different things. You're in love—that's great. But that doesn't mean the rest of your life needs to suffer. It worries us that you say you're miserable when you're not with him. Life is so full of things to do and people to spend time with, and you don't want to mess up the rest of your life because you're so devoted to your boyfriend. We hate to tell you this, but it's not really healthy to be this focused on one person. You may want to spend every last minute with him, but don't! Pursue other hobbies and hang with friends a few times every week. Having an outside life will keep you from seeming desperate (which is a turnoff anyway). Plus, if things do end, you won't be stranded.

Q "His birthday's coming and I'd really like to get my boyfriend something special. The thing is, we've only been together about a month. It hasn't gotten serious yet, but that doesn't mean I want to get him something insignificant. What if the relationship ends up really taking off? Are there any gift-giving guidelines I can follow?"

A At this stage, it's hard to tell if he'll become a long-term boyfriend. So you want to give him a gift that lets him know you're open to more—but that you're not trying to rush him into a big romance. Surprise him casually with something small and simple—and under $25. Is there a movie he's mentioned he likes a lot? Why not see if it's out on DVD. As things progress, so can your gift commitment. Treat him to something he wouldn't buy for himself that will: (1) show him you really "get him" and (2) tell him you're looking forward to more great times. When you've been together for a while, and the relationship looks more serious, that's when to pull out all the stops. At this point, you already know that this guy deserves something special. Since you both realize that this relationship is serious, you're in the clear to go with a gift that's sentimental or to make plans for an activity that you can look forward to together. Maybe you can buy him a nice watch he's been eyeing, or plan an elegant dinner date at a swanky new restaurant. Just remember—the gift you give never has to cost a lot. Being a good girlfriend to him by making the day special is the most important thing.

A PeRfEcT RoMaNcE

Q "I love my boyfriend, but it seems like every time we do something, it's always something he wants to do. When we first started dating, he always asked me what I wanted to do, and it seemed to be more equal. Now it's just him, him, him! I feel like I've lost control in this relationship. How can I get it back?"

A That's easy. Sometimes you need to put yourself first. This isn't about bossing him around, it's about remembering who you are, what you like, and why you're so loveable. Don't start bailing on your friends to see him. And do keep running cross country, loving heavy metal—even if he hates it—or doing whatever it is that makes you *you*. Not only do these things renew your confidence in yourself, they remind him of why he wanted to be (and why he is so lucky to be) with you in the first place! If he never wants to do what you want to do, that may be the sign of another problem in the relationship: that you're starting to grow apart. You should both be enjoying yourself here. If he never wants to see your favorite band or hang out with your friends, maybe it's time to start hanging out with someone who will!

CG! TIP: Hide a cute note in his homework. The surprise will put a smile on his face and show him how much you care!

Q "I sometimes feel like my boyfriend doesn't really love me because he doesn't like to answer me when I ask him how I look. If he cared, wouldn't he always reassure me that I look great?"

A When you ask a guy about your looks, he sees a trap, and often times, he'll shut down. If you've been together for a while and feel comfortable with each other, it's okay to ask him if he likes your shirt or if you look good. But, if you constantly need his opinion to feel good about yourself, you need to learn to be confident from within. When you are, you'll look and feel better and he'll respond to that.

CG! TIP: When's the best time to tell him you love him? Pick a special, shared moment. If he's the right guy, he'll be happy you opened up.

A PeRfEcT RoMaNcE

Q "I've been dating my boyfriend for three years now, but it hasn't exactly been perfect. He lies to me—a lot. He has some friends I don't really approve of and he never tells me the truth about when he sees them or what they do together. Still, it really hurts my feelings when he lies. How can I get him to stop?"

A If you want honesty, you can't yell at him when he tells you stuff you don't want to hear—you've got to at least commend him for being upfront, you know? And as much as it drives you crazy, he does have the right to choose his own friends. What you guys need is to write out a "Must List"—the top five things you must have in a partner. A small issue to one person may be huge to the other. Talk honestly about how you can meet each other's needs without compromising your own. If you can reach this middle ground and honor it, the two of you will probably make it. If you can't, now might be the time to cut bait before the relationship gets any more serious. If you aren't compatible now, you're not going to grow into compatibility as a couple—it just doesn't work that way. And the longer you drag out a relationship that doesn't work, the more painful it's going to be to end. If you can't accept him for who he is, you need to find someone who you can accept—and who accepts you, just as you are.

Q **"I can't get my boyfriend to make the first move to kiss me. When I kiss him, he always responds so I know he's into it...but how can I get him to initiate?"**

A Believe it or not, some guys may be too shy to take the initiative. And that's the way it sounds with your guy. Here's an idea to get things going without intimidating him. Invite him over to watch a romantic comedy with you. When a kissing scene comes on, lean over to him, smile, and slyly say, "We should try that." See what he does. Chances are, he'll be feeling comfortable enough to kiss you because he knows you want him to!

A PeRfEcT RoMaNcE

Q "I love my boyfriend, but I hate kissing him. Well, it's not that I hate kissing him, but his kisses are always so sloppy and wet. What can I do to help him be a better kisser without hurting his feelings?"

A Maybe you could try a little humor with your guy. When he kisses you the way you don't like, pull away, wipe your face in an obvious way, and make a joke like this: "Whoa—we're drenching each other!" You could also try saying something like "We're such goofballs—let's ease up on the saliva!" When you make it about the both of you, he won't think you're blaming it all on him and you'll also get your message across!

CG! TIP: Give your guy sweet butterfly kisses, it's a fun variation that'll make you both laugh.

Q **"Sometimes when my boyfriend kisses me, he jams his tongue way too far in the back of my mouth and it feels like I'm going to choke to death. Help!"**

A The real secret to being a good kisser is knowing how to handle the not-so-sexy moments that sometimes crop up—and that means handling them with sensitivity. The next time your guy tries to lick your tonsils, create some distance by subtly pulling back from the kiss. Then pause, put your hands on his shoulders to keep him a bit farther away and restart the kiss with you guiding the action. That should be enough to turn his awkward kiss into romantic bliss!

CG! TIP: Offer to walk your guy's dog. Caring for his "best friend" shows him that you care about him.

Chapter 3

is he a good match... or a bad catch?

You've got this guy, but for some reason the relationship isn't what you expected it to be. Should you stick around and see if you can work things out—or should you send him packing? Check out how we've helped other CosmoGIRL!s deal with this dilemma.

GoOd MaTcH?

Q "I really like my boyfriend, but I have a hard time trusting guys. I've been cheated on before, and I'm always waiting for it to happen with every new guy. This guy seems different. He's always there when I need him and he's never cheated on a girlfriend before, but I can't help but be worried that it's going to happen to me again. What should I do?"

A The most important thing we can tell you: Leave your past in your past. While it's okay to be cautious when getting involved with a new guy, it's unfair to compare everyone to that jerk who broke your heart. It sounds to us like your guy is really respectful, and that's the key to trust. Need a ride? He'll show up—on time. Want to talk? He'll be there—in full support mode. We don't have ESP or anything, but it doesn't look like this guy would betray you. Congrats! We think you've found a truly great guy!

CG! TIP: If a guy gets to be called your boyfriend, he should make your life enjoyable, not miserable!

Q "My boyfriend makes me mad a lot. He breaks dates and sometimes he doesn't call me for days at a time. The problem is, I can't seem to stay mad at him. While he doesn't always apologize for upsetting me, he gives me these puppy dog eyes and I just melt. I can't help myself. I know I should stay angry at least until he apologizes or something. What should I do?"

A A guy who can't admit he's wrong and apologize to you when he hurts you is just not worth wasting your time on. Sure he does that cute basset hound thing with his eyes. But really think about whether you should trust him. You've noticed that he misses commitments and breaks rules, and that shows that he's immature. Not to be harsh (look, we know it's tempting to like bad boys), but if you keep going out with this guy, you may really get hurt. Why not try looking for someone who's more respectful instead— someone who respects you and who you know you can count on. After all, you deserve it!

CG! TIP: If a guy gets in trouble for bad behavior a lot, take it as a warning sign that he might not be good for you.

GoOd MaTcH?

Q "I like this guy who's sweet and funny and everything I want in a guy, but he smokes pot. It's a big deal to me. Because of my morals, I never do pot. But I really like him. Should I just look the other way?"

A In a word: No! And in more words: You should never let your morals slide—especially about an issue that could affect your safety (and is—ahem—illegal). It's one thing to compromise on little things when you're in a relationship (all relationships need some give-and-take), but there's no reason to compromise yourself to make a relationship happen. Trust that instinct of yours: It's never going to feel right if you "let it slide" that he smokes pot. No guy is perfect—but if you start a relationship by overlooking something so important to you, it'll pave the way for you to let more things slide and, ultimately, to settle for less than you want. And worse, you'll end up trying to change him—or be in situations where you feel pressured to do things you don't want to do. It's hard to hear, but your best bet is to give up on this guy and hold out for one who has the traits you admire but who doesn't smoke pot. Because when you set your standards high and stick to them, people will rise to the occasion. That's the kind of person you deserve.

CG! TIP: A good boyfriend encourages you to achieve your goals—and is proud of you when you do.

Q "I really like my boyfriend, but I sometimes feel like I'm more into the relationship than he is. I feel like it's me who's always calling him, and that I'm always arranging our get-togethers. He always talks to me when I call and goes along with the dates I plan, but is that really enough?"

A It looks like this guy doesn't want to lift a finger in this relationship and you deserve much more. Hard as it may be, tell him, "I really like you, but I feel like you're not into this and it's bumming me out. If you're not willing to contribute to this relationship as much as I am, I don't want to be in it anymore." You'll know from his response if he's willing to shape up, or if you should ship him out of your life.

CG! TIP: Don't put your guy up on a pedestal. No one should be worshipped. You just want to be able to relate to and have fun with each other.

GoOd MaTcH?

Q "I met this guy this summer and we're having a really great time together. The problem is, he's from Ireland, just visiting for the summer, and he doesn't have any future plans to come back to the States. I really like him. Do you think there's any way we can make it work as a more serious relationship?"

A Distance creates problems in even the most serious relationships—and that's even when couples make plans to see one another regularly. Looks like you probably won't see your Irish cutie again for a long time—if at all. By not expressing interest in coming back to the States, he's telling you that he's not interested in pursuing this relationship past the summer romance stage. So for him, it may just be a fling. If knowing that hurts too much for you, maybe you should cut your losses and break off the romance now. But if you know it's going to end and feel okay about that, why not savor it while you have it—and then enjoy the memories.

CG! TIP: If your guy opens up to you, never use his secrets against him in a fight. If you do, he'll think he can't trust you again.

Q "I met a guy this summer who worked as a counselor in the same camp as me. We both just learned that we're planning to attend the same college. I'm excited about it and hope he's excited too. (I'm just not sure!) I want our summer fling to grow into something more, but is a fling always just a fling?"

A Sounds to us like this has the potential to become something serious. Even though it seemed like this would be a temporary thing, the fact that you have the opportunity to open a new chapter of your lives together means you have a chance to grow and develop your relationship on a whole new level! Not sure he shares your enthusiasm? Take a risk by asking him, "What do you think will happen with us?" or just see where the relationship goes once you start school.

GoOd MaTcH?

Q "I met this guy over the summer and we really hit it off. We've spent just about every day together, and it just feels so natural. The problem is, he's going back to school in California at the end of August—and I'm on the East Coast. Can we keep the romance alive?"

A You may not have been looking for something serious with your summer fling, but if you've been spending that much time together, chances are you've found something. But long distance relationships are really tough—especially when you're in college and experiencing all kinds of new things at once. It will take a lot of effort from both of you to survive the separation, but these things have been known to work. The only advice we can give you for now is to keep communicating openly, and your summer love will have a better chance to keep burning.

Q "I met this guy at a party. We danced and talked all night and I thought we really hit it off. He even asked me for my number. But that was weeks ago, and he hasn't called. What went wrong?"

A We're not trying to be mean here, but the truth is that lots of guys ask for numbers when they can't handle the pressure of saying goodbye. By asking for it after you've been by his side all night, he gets to look nice, whether he plans on calling or not. How can you be sure a guy really wants to call you? Next time you meet someone you like, just talk to him for 20 minutes or so, then go hang out with your friends. This will take the pressure off him. As you're leaving, say it was great meeting him. If he asks, give him your number. This way, you'll know he's not asking because he thinks, "We've hung out all night, I should get her number." He's asking because he really wants to call you. Brring!

Q **"There's this guy I know who wants to hang out with me sometimes, like when I'm babysitting, to make out, but when I see him in school, he treats me like he barely even knows I exist. It really bothers me. What should I do?"**

A You say it bothers you and you're absolutely right that it should. Why is he giving you the cold shoulder in public, but then turning the heat to high when it's just the two of you? Essentially, it looks to us like he doesn't want to seem attached— either because his friends will say he's "whipped" (guys hate being teased) or because he wants other girls to think he's available. He likes you (and definitely likes kissing you), but he also wants to keep his options open. Our advice? Don't hook up, hang out alone, or call him until he changes his ways in public. Ask if he wants to hang out with you and some friends this weekend. If he misses you, he'll say yes. But if he doesn't, give this player up. That way, you're the one making the rules.

GoOd MaTcH?

Q "I like this guy, but he's involved with another girl. I know he's not happy with her. Lately he's been confiding in me a lot and the other day, he even made a move on me. I want to date him. How can I talk him into breaking up with her and being with me?"

A First of all, you need to step back and ask yourself if you really want him. He doesn't respect either one of you enough to think of your feelings. He's either a bad guy, or he's a good guy who just hasn't figured out yet that girls are actually people. By sticking with him, you're saying that you're only worthy of half a boyfriend. Show him how respectable you are by respecting yourself: Don't get involved with him as long as he's with her. Even if he breaks up and swears he loves you, keep your guard up until you're positive he means it.

CG! TIP: Communication in a relationship is key. If you don't talk to each other openly, it's never going to work out.

Q "There's this kid who I like—well, love—but I'm never happy talking to him. So I told him that I didn't want to talk to him anymore. I've been crying day and night, and it doesn't even seem to bother him. Should I tell him that I want to talk to him again?"

A We girls always complain about guys playing games, but your situation sounds like the opposite. It sounds as if you didn't like how he was treating you, so you decided to "punish" him by telling him that you didn't want to talk to him anymore, and now you're upset that he's not upset. Ask yourself why you told him that you wanted to stop talking to him: Were you really serious—or was it just to get a reaction from him? If you truly did want to stop talking to him, then give yourself time—it's tough to stop spending time with someone you like. But if you just wanted to get a reaction from him, then you went the wrong way. If a guy isn't treating you how you want, it may be that not every guy you like feels the same way about you. Guys who are into you treat you well—don't fool yourself into thinking otherwise. You have to move on and find a guy who you won't have to play games with. Yes, it's easier said than done, but it's the only way you'll get into a truly healthy relationship. Don't create a big drama out of it. Move on with your life, have fun with friends, and soon enough you'll find a guy who will give you the attention you need.

GoOd MaTcH?

Q "I've been talking to this guy online and off. We really hit it off, but he lives like 200 miles away. I would do anything to be with him. What should I do?"

A You're being casual about two things we just can't ignore. When you say you'd do "anything" to be with this guy—that puts you in a bad place because you're saying you don't have boundaries—which you need to maintain your sense of self. The other is the Internet relationship thing. Sure, lots of people have met online and started relationships. But there are also perverts out there who will take advantage of girls who are kindhearted enough to trust openly. Sweet as he may seem, take precautions. Tell him you want to see his driver's license pic and have him email it to you. Then call his state police department to find out how to check if someone is a convicted sex offender. We want you to be safe! With that out of the way, our advice is don't rush it. Don't make any drastic moves (like relocating). Keep asking lots of questions so you can really get to know him. If after a month, you decide that you still like him, then plan a trip. Each should gather a few friends and meet up one afternoon. Go somewhere fun and public that's midway between your homes. Even after the trip, keep taking it slow. If it's meant to be, you won't lose him just by taking your time—you'll allow your relationship to blossom naturally.

CG! TIP: The best way to meet guys is through mutual friends or acquaintances. Keep your guard up when you meet a guy online or out of the blue.

Q "My boyfriend and I have been dating only three months and I'm feeling taken for granted. Before we started going out, we were great friends and I think he still treats me like I'm just a friend. He talks to me like I'm one of the guys, and sometimes he puts me on hold to answer another call and doesn't come back to talk to me right away. I like him a lot, but I wish he could be more serious with me. What should I do?"

A People don't change overnight, so if your boyfriend's always been casual and goofy with you, you can't expect that he's all of a sudden going to turn into a prince charming. But, you deserve respect, so if you think you're not getting it, you probably aren't. The way we see it, you might just be better off as friends.

CG! TIP: Stop worrying about whether or not he thinks you're right for him—start asking yourself if *he's* right for *you*!

GoOd MaTcH?

Q "My boyfriend is very emotional. He cries a lot and treats me like I'm his world. I don't think it's healthy for a 19-year-old guy to act this way. What do you think?"

A It's not healthy for anybody to be dependent on someone else for their happiness. One thing you can do is encourage him to go out with his friends. If he doesn't have many friends, talk to him about what his other interests are. Once you see what he's interested in, get excited about and involved in them. He'll meet new people and be in a world that doesn't just revolve around you. The other thing you can do is make plans without him. That will give him (and you) space, so he can learn to fill his time with other things. But don't avoid him—that would be mean. Just start focusing on your own life and encourage him to do the same. If he freaks out at these suggestions, then you've got to have a talk. Right now, his biggest fear is that you'll leave him. Tell him that as much as you care about him, you feel he's too dependent on you, and it puts a lot of pressure on you to keep him happy. In the end, you have to live your life for yourself—no one else. You can help your boyfriend see that—but in the end, it's his responsibility to get himself there.

CG! TIP: Rather than worrying about what may happen if you and your guy break up, try to think of it as an opportunity to savor being single as well as spend quality time with your friends (and develop new crushes!).

Q "I've been with my boyfriend for a long time. He's not that attractive, but he has the coolest personality (and not to be conceited, but I'm pretty attractive, so I can't see him cheating on me). But we were at a party and a girl grabbed his butt as she walked by. Ever since, I'm worried he's cheating on me. He's even had new girls' numbers in his cell phone lately. Am I misreading the situation?"

A It sounds like you may have more issues with this guy than some girl acting inappropriately around him. Actually, the biggest issue you seem to have is trust. Just because someone takes an interest in your boyfriend doesn't mean that he's interested in her. You say you're an attractive girl, which means that guys probably flirt with you too. Does that mean you're hooking up with every guy who flirts with you? Of course not. So why should it be different for him? Now the thing about the numbers in the cell phone is one we can't really answer fully because we don't know him. If you suspect he's cheating on you, the best way to find out is to just confront him with it. Just be prepared to know the truth.

CG! TIP: Trust is the most important part of any relationship. Without it, there is no relationship.

ChAPTeR 4

breaking up
for smarties

It looked like you and your guy were on the right track, and then all of a sudden, WHAM! You broke up. What's a CosmoGIRL! to do? Read on and find out!

BrEakinG up for SmaRties

Q "My boyfriend just broke up with me last week but I'm still in love with him. How can I get him back?"

A We hate to tell you this, but we'd say this game is over. There are reasons that people don't stay together, and they usually make a lot of sense in time. When emotions are running high, it might not be easy to be rational about what's going on, but when time has a chance to heal broken hearts, breakups tend to make more sense. In fact, it's very rare that when people break up that they can happily get back together. Now, that said, we're going to tell you something else you probably don't want to hear: It's easier to get someone back if you were the one who did the dumping, but even then there are no guarantees. Apologizing for making a huge mistake is much easier to do than convincing someone who may no longer love you that they actually do. Our advice? Try your best to move on. There are so many guys out there who may get along with you better than this guy ever did, CosmoGIRL! And that makes for a much better match than someone who was so ambivalent about being with you that he broke your heart. You need a guy who *wants* to be with you, not someone you need to convince! So pick yourself up and get ready to meet a guy who's really right for you!

CG! TIP: Want to get your ex back? Try giving him space. If it's meant to be, he'll miss you soon enough and come back for you.

Q "A few months ago, my ex-boyfriend and I had a big fight and broke up. Lately, I really find myself wishing we could get back together. We're talking again now and he even asked me to have dinner with him. Is it possible that we could be getting back together?"

A It's obvious that you still care about him, and if he's looking to have a date with you, it may be that he still has romantic feelings for you, too. But if you decide to get back together, we encourage you enough to have "The Talk": Discuss what each of you can do differently this time around so you can get beyond the problems that broke you up in the first place. One of the big problems in many relationships is lack of communication. No matter how big a fight couples have, it's essential to the health of the relationship to talk things through, which you guys are figuring out now. If you communicate properly this time around, chances are you won't fall into the same ruts again and you can make it work this time. Now, if he's still into you, but he's not sure about getting back together, keep your options open. Be patient and open to new experiences (and guys), and focus on building a new relationship with him—a friendship. It'll be a good foundation if you two ever decide to take things back to a romantic level.

CG! TIP: Think of love—and the pain of breaking up—as exercise for your heart. The pain is tough, but it only means your heart is getting stronger.

BrEakinG up for SmaRties

Q "I'm having trouble with my ex. We keep trying to work things out, but he gets almost crazy and obsessive sometimes—he scares me a little. But I still care about him a lot because he treats me like a princess when we're together. Without him, I'm lonely. What should I do?"

A Be patient, because one day, you will have a relationship with a guy who treats you like a strong, solid woman—not a princess, which isn't really healthy. We hate to tell you this, but it's time to move on. Maybe you're just staying with this guy because you're trying to avoid being lonely. But the truth is, you can be more lonely sticking with the wrong guy than you can by just being by yourself. If you stay with him, you can expect more of the tears and bad feelings you had the first time you were together. If you break up with him once and for all, you'll at last open the door for a new love to enter your life!

CG! TIP: Relationships take two people to make them work. You can only control your actions—not anyone else's.

Q "My boyfriend just broke up with me after six months together, and he's already with someone else. He always talks about her, and I don't know what to say back, so I lied and said I had a boyfriend. Now I feel guilty. Should I tell him the truth?"

A We think you should stop telling this guy anything. You need to change your focus—from him back to you. We know it's hard to watch him go on with his life. But, whether or not you like it: He's with someone else, not you. Once you start accepting that, we guarantee you'll be able to move on too. Now don't force yourself to get over him right this second. You have to give yourself some time to heal (there's no magic formula, but most people need about one week for every month they were with a guy). The key to getting on with your life is to use that time to get back in touch with you. So instead of sitting around pining for him, spend your energy doing things—as in not him-related things. And what should you do about your little new-boyfriend lie? Nothing. It's time to move on, quietly. Don't feel guilty, and don't create new reasons to talk to your ex-boyfriend. Get over him knowing that you've got the strength of a million CosmoGIRL!s who have your back!

CG! TIP: Don't get down on love if a relationship doesn't work out. You will eventually find the guy you're supposed to be with—even if you have to kiss a lot of frogs first!

BrEakinG up for SmaRties

Q "I loved this guy forever and when he asked me out a few months ago, I felt like I had everything I ever needed. Problem is, it didn't work out. He recently broke my heart and now I feel all empty inside again. What should I do?"

A First of all, remember that a guy who deserves your love should think you're amazing. If he doesn't and you're still crying over him, you're focused on the wrong thing—how cute or cool he is, and how being with him makes you feel valuable. So what should you do? You need to get more in touch with yourself. For months—or years—you equated your self-worth with whether or not this guy you worshipped would like you. When you "got" him, your self-esteem shot up like a rocket. Because you put your sense of value onto this guy liking you, you felt great when he did. When he didn't anymore, and things with him didn't work out, you lost your sense of value, and that's not good. You can't measure your self-worth in what others think of you—whether that means a boy, a teacher, an employer, or whomever else. Your sense of self-worth has to come from within. When you put the focus back on yourself, when you firmly believe in yourself as being an awesome person (without relying on anyone or anything else to prove it to you) then it can't be stripped away from you. You'll end up *wanting* approval, instead of *needing* it, which means you'll never be left feeling empty.

Q "I just had my first real relationship and it was wonderful. So much so that even though I knew he was going off to college, it didn't occur to me that we'd have to break up. And then one night, out of nowhere, he just blurted out: 'I think we should see other people.' I was so shocked, I couldn't even speak. I just stood up and left. Now I feel unresolved about the whole thing. Will I ever feel better?"

A It's a common scenario—getting dumped out of the blue. And if it happens to you, it leaves you wondering, What did I do wrong? To help put your mind at ease, take heart that the answer for what you did wrong is *nothing*. You just got so excited to get on the roller coaster of love that you forgot to pull down the safety harness, and now you're stuck learning a few things the hard way. You wouldn't allow yourself to see the possibility that the relationship might end when he left for college, so it hit you like a ton of bricks when it actually happened. Don't worry: You can prevent that from happening again. Just remember to proceed with caution the next time you fall in love. The ride will be just as much fun—only much safer!

Q "I was with my boyfriend for two months when he decided he didn't like me anymore. I was heartbroken. Then, two weeks later, he called and told me everything he didn't like about me. He said I was ugly, that I'm annoying and loud, and only guys are allowed to be loud and annoying. I am still really hurting from his attack. How can I make sure nothing like this ever happens to me again?"

A We hate to tell you this, but you can't control the behavior of others, so there is no way to be sure that *nothing* like this will ever happen to you again. But you can take some precautions. It's obvious to you now that this guy was a jerk, but when you were in love, your judgment was probably impaired because you may not have taken enough time getting to know him. If you had taken it slower, you may have realized he was a jerk—and dumped him before he had the chance to hurt you. The next time you fall in love, take your time. You'll never know one hundred percent if a guy will break your heart, but the more you know him before you develop strong feelings for him, the better!

CG! TIP: When your heart's been broken, take a break from dating. You'll have a chance to get back in touch with yourself, and figure out what you're really looking for from your next relationship.

Q "About three weeks ago, a guy asked me out. Then within just a couple of days, he dumped me. He said he wasn't ready for a relationship. He kept saying it wasn't my fault, and he was stupid. I was really mad at him because I still really like him. What should I do?"

A No matter what the situation, you'll never have control over what another person is thinking—and that goes especially for dating. All you can do is keep your ears open to try to be sure he wants to be with you as much as you want to be with him when he asks you out. And if he doesn't? Say goodbye so you can find the smarty who does. As far as this guy goes, know that the problem is totally his and not yours. It was immature of him to ask you out and then right away take it back because he didn't want to be involved. You deserve much better than that!

CG! TIP: Keep upbeat and positive. There's nothing hotter than a happy, confident person!

BrEakinG up for SmaRties

Q "I broke up with my ex two months ago, and he still wants to know my every move. He gets mad when he finds out I'm with another guy, even if it's just a friend. How can I get him to let go?"

A This is not good—for you or for him. Have you had an honest talk with him? If not, you need to make it clear that it's really over. Be polite, honest, and brief—and don't accuse him of anything (that'll just start a fight). Tell him you're really uncomfortable with his keeping tabs on you and getting angry about other guys. If he denies doing it, say that you don't want to argue but that it's important that he lets you go. If he still denies it, just say, "Okay, I'm glad it's not an issue." And say goodbye. If he starts acting creepy (like following you, or threatening you—even remotely), get serious and take action. Write down everything he's done that's made you uncomfortable. Stalking is illegal—so report it to your school, or to an adult you can talk to. If that doesn't straighten things out, tell your parents and file a police report. And if you ever feel at risk physically, call 911 right away. Anything is possible, so it's important to be prepared. Use your judgment, listen to your gut, and handle the situation in a very direct, strong way. No one has the right to impose on your freedom.

Q "My boyfriend just broke up with me and I feel like no one will ever go out with me again. Will I ever find a new guy?"

A Everyone feels this way at one time or another in their lives, and guess what? Most everyone eventually finds someone new. But if you want to speed up the process, you have to put yourself out there. You don't have to be a desperate girl who never stays home for fear she'll miss a boy-meeting opportunity. Just don't be afraid to bring a book to a café, or to hit the park with your guitar. Put yourself in places where you won't see the same old guys who aren't doing it for you. Go to places where the right guy will wonder, "Who's that girl?" Now, you already know you're loveable, and you should have confidence in that. If you're walking around radiating "I'm never going to find love," guess what? You're never going to find love. Tell yourself you deserve to find love and you will. Your thoughts affect your behavior, and your behavior is what people respond to. Do something today that puts a positive "I rock and you want to be part of my world!" spring in your step and it will attract cool people—including guys—to you. Finally, stop waiting for the perfect guy to come into your life. Once you stop focusing about whether or not you'll find him, you'll be more fun to be with. And that's when Mr. Right will find you. So stop wasting your time thinking. Instead, put your energy into the fun you can have today, and soon you'll see love rolling out for you like a red carpet.

Breaking up for Smarties

Q "When I was sixteen, I dated this guy for almost a year. He was my first and only love. It's been more than two years since we broke up, and it still hurts. He totally destroyed my faith in the opposite sex, and now it's hard for me to trust any guy. I just want to know how to get over the pain of being hurt and how to break down the barrier I've built up since my heartbreak so that I can let in someone new."

A You say you want to get over him, but that's hard if in the back of your head, you still have feelings about getting him back. If you do want to get over him, you have to get rid of reminders of him—his football jersey, the teddy bear he won for you, all of it. In the trash. Yes, it's hard. But it'll be impossible to forget about him if there are mementos from your relationship lying around. Next, go away somewhere by yourself (if your parents let you). Just go on an overnight trip somewhere close by, like an inn on the shore—whatever feels like it's a world away. Before you go, make sure you pack: super-comfortable clothes, a scented candle, a great body cream, and a brand-new journal. When you arrive, go for a walk, look at the scenery, and let it inspire you. Dream about all the things you want for yourself. Then go back to your room, light that candle, take a nice long shower, put on the yummy body lotion, get into bed, and write.

What do you deserve? What are the traits that any guy who's worth your time has to have? Just let it flow. (And if you can't actually get away, go to the nearest park or beach to clear your mind and let yourself be inspired—and then light that candle at home and write!) The more you focus on you, the less you'll focus on him, and the more confident you'll be.

CG! TIP: Plan an "over him" party with your friends. Bring ex-boyfriend photos and make confetti out of them! It'll give you closure.

Q "I've made a totally dumb mistake for ending things with my guy! He was always willing to do things to make me happy. Instead of appreciating that, I felt like I wanted more excitement. Now I realize that we had a great thing going. How can I get him back?"

A It seems like you've fallen into the "he's too nice" trap. The truth is, sometimes it's hard to realize how good you had it until it's gone. It's helpful to get a guy's perspective on how he's feeling and what it would take to get him back. Talk to your guy friends about how they would respond in a similar situation. Take the advice that sounds most helpful, and good luck! Remember, if nothing works at getting your ex back, think of this as a growing experience for you, and use what you've learned in your future relationships.

ChAPTeR 5

you and your
guy friends

Sure they can make great friends—and sometimes they
can be a whole lot more! Read on and see how other
CosmoGIRL!s relate to their guy pals.

GuY FrIeNdS

Q "I have guy friends who say that I'm butch because I like wearing Bermuda shorts and T-shirts. I try to wear make-up sometimes, but they still think I need a makeover. Should I change to please them?"

A No way! We don't want to sound cliché when we say this but, here goes: You should never change yourself just to please someone else. We know you like these guys, and they're probably great friends in lots of ways, so we're not going to say you shouldn't hang out with them or anything. But we do hope that you'll stick up for yourself when they say this stuff in the future. Next time they bug you about the way you dress, tell them you like your Bermuda shorts and feel like yourself in them. On top of that, they're comfortable (and between us girls, who wants to be picking at wedgies all day because the tight pants you're wearing mean you have to wear a thong?). While your guy friends may like girls to dress a certain way, it's not like you need to turn yourself into their Barbie doll. If you don't want to wear makeup—fine. As long as you like yourself, that's what really matters. After all, it's our differences that make us interesting.

CG! TIP: Never change your appearance to please someone else, especially not a guy. When you look and feel comfortable in your own skin, the right guys will notice that.

Q "I recently made out with one of my best guy friends. It was really great and we really connected. The problem is, he has a girlfriend. They've been dating for a few years but have been playing each other the whole time. We both like each other, but now I don't know how to act around him. What should I do?"

A Ever had a friend who you connect with so well you feel like you should be more than just friends. And we know from experience that good friends can make good boyfriends. But don't settle for sharing him. You need to ask yourself what you really want. If you want to date your friend, you'll have to tell him "Her or me." If he chooses her, your friendship doesn't stand much of a chance, no matter how mature you both are. And if he chooses you, you'll always wonder if he'll cheat on you like he did with his other girlfriend. (For the record, while it's not your job to keep a guy from cheating on his girlfriend, you don't have to be an accomplice either.) If you decide dating isn't worth risking your friendship, you're still facing a long conversation and a lot of work to get a platonic friendship back on track. These decisions are not fun, but it's better than wondering, "What if?" And keep in mind, do you want to be with a guy who cheats on his girlfriend? You deserve a real relationship; don't settle for being a booty call.

GuY FrIeNdS

Q "I have a really close guy friend who I've known since we were kids, but lately I've been feeling some intense romantic feelings for him. I'm starting to think he feels the same about me. In fact, the other day, it felt like we were going to kiss—but we didn't. He spends a lot of time with me, but he really hasn't put any moves on me. So what should I do?"

A It sounds as though he may also care for you in a deeper way and might want things to turn romantic. But maybe he can't tell how you feel about him, so he's keeping his options open. Pay close attention to what's going on—on both sides, not just yours. If you don't feel a spark from him after all, then just relax and enjoy your friendship if you can. Maybe even ease up on the time you spend together to help let your feelings cool off a bit. But if you do get a strong sense that he's into you too—like that intense almost-kissing moment—maybe it's time to take a chance. Wait until you're hanging out alone and ask, "Have you ever thought about the possibility of an 'us'?" Then take it from there and see if that almost-kiss turns into a full-fledged lip-lock.

Q **"This may sound conceited, but I think my best guy friend has a big crush on me. He's always looking at me with this dopey look on his face, and lately he spends more time with me than ever before. What should I do?"**

A Looks like someone's smitten—and it's him! Yes, it seems like he totally has the hots for you. If you feel the same, tell him! But if the thought of kissing him is as appealing as kissing your brother (ew!), give him hints that you're not looking to him for love (ask some other guy friends for advice). Try saying, "I'm picking up signals that you want more than friendship, but I don't feel the same. Can we stick to being friends?" If he feels rejected, give him space to focus on finding someone else.

CG! TIP: A guy isn't always up for making the first move (maybe he's super shy or afraid his friends will make fun of him). So just because he hasn't approached you doesn't mean he doesn't like you.

GuY FrIeNdS

Q "One of my guy friends keeps asking me out, but I don't like him like that, and I really don't want to ruin our friendship. What should I tell him when he asks me out again?"

A Guys don't chase after girls they truly believe they have no shot with. They have egos! Make sure you haven't been leading this guy on without realizing it. It's very flattering to be pursued, and it's normal to want to keep him hanging around. If you genuinely want him to stop pursuing you, be direct. Not in a mean way, but in an honest way. Say something like, "I'm so flattered that you like me romantically, but that's not how I see us. I do want to be your friend, but for us to really be friends, you'll need to respect that our relationship will never go beyond friendship." You need to be honest—and clear— with the guy, especially if you want to save your friendship.

CG! TIP: Get to know a new guy by going out in a group. Do something silly like bowling or mini golf, so there's no pressure on you to be alone or serious.

Q "I'm starting to have romantic feelings for my guy friend, but I don't know if he likes me too. Sure we hang out all the time and we confide in each other about lots of things—but sometimes he talks to me about other girls. Is there a chance he likes me the same way I like him?"

A It seems he likes you as a really close friend. He thinks of you as family because you have fun together and because you're always there when things get tough. It doesn't look like there's a romance here because he seems to be looking for pointers from you about dating other girls. While he seems to think of you as a great pal, he doesn't think of you as a girlfriend right now. He counts on you the same way he counts on his other friends—to hang out, crack each other up, and get love advice. So enjoy your friendship for what it is: You two are lucky to have each other to depend on. And listen, his feelings for you may turn romantic one day, but for now, that's just not how he sees you. If you try to read more into his actions, you could get hurt.

CG! TIP: Want a guy to know you're into him? Tell him with your body language. Touch his arms gently while you talk to him and look him in the eye. He'll get the idea!

GuY FrIeNdS

Q "I made a new guy friend at the beginning of the school year, but it seems to have grown into much more than that. We spend a lot of time together and talk on the phone for hours every night. The other day, he bought a shirt and wore it out of the store just because I said I liked it. I really like him and think he may feel the same. Could there be more than a friendship here?"

A You're right: This guy sees you as way more than a friend—you seem to spark something in him. Maybe he can't explain it, but it's just the way he feels when you're around (you bring out a side of him no one else does—including a new appreciation for fashion!). It looks like you have a chemistry with this guy that's landed you a spot in his heart. Enjoy it! Try to show him the same understanding, respect, and affection he gives to you, and see where your relationship goes.

CG! TIP: Guys like to feel smart and helpful, so ask him questions about something he's into.

Q "Two years ago, my best friend's girlfriend broke up with him, and he was devastated. About three months later, he and I hooked up for two weeks, and then he broke up with me. Later, he told me that he cheated on me. Now he and I want things to be the way they were before we went out. But every time I hang out with him, I get filled with rage and either end up crying or yelling at him. I don't know what to do."

A When you started dating your friend, you opened your relationship to new terrain, which can be great when things are going well or not so great. In the past, if he cheated on a girlfriend, it wasn't hurting you. But now, he has hurt you, and as much as you want to be friends, it may not be possible—at least not for a while. It's normal for you to still be upset with him—you wouldn't be human if you weren't. Try writing him a letter telling him exactly how you feel. Then fold up the letter and put it away: You're writing it for *your* benefit, not *his*. You need to get all those emotions out so you can make peace with what's happened. Once you let go of your anger, you can build a new and different friendship with him, if that's what you still want. It may be a little less close than before, but that's to be expected. Betrayal is an extremely hard thing to get over. But hopefully you can start taking those steps towards healing.

CG! TIP: Great friends don't always make great boyfriends—and vice versa.

ChApTeR 6

guys and your family

They say they only want what's best for you, but why
does it seem like your family is always getting in the
way when it comes to you and guys? Read on and see
what dilemmas and questions other CosmoGIRL!s
have had!

Q "I was taught that interracial dating is wrong. Now a co-worker—who happens to be black—and I are into each other. How can I go out with him without upsetting my family? Help!"

A Treat this relationship the way you would treat any new relationship, regardless of race: Get to know this guy for a few weeks, and if things go well, that's when you'll want to tell your parents. At that point, say, "My parents might not be happy about us dating, but I need to tell them. Will you stand by me while I work things out with them?" If he's not up for it, that's the end of the relationship. Because if you sneak around, it will put a lot of stress on you and the guy, which could cause you to break up anyway. Plus, it will damage your relationship with your parents, since they'll sense you pulling away from them. But if he is willing to stand by you, tell your parents you're interested in this guy who happens to be black. Say that you'd like them to meet him before they fall back on their "no interracial dating" rule. If they still can't see past his race, explain that you've become more open-minded, and while you respect their values, you'd like them to respect yours, even though they're different. Ultimately, you may have to abide by their rules. But know that your open-mindedness will serve you well in the future when you're the only one making decisions for you.

Q **"My dad refuses to accept my relationship with my boyfriend of two years. We've tried to talk to him calmly many times, but it never seems to matter. How can we make him see that we're right for each other and that he should give us his blessing?"**

A Sometimes dads have a hard time accepting their little girls are all grown up and ready to date boys. It's not unusual for a father to be protective over his daughter, but usually when dad gets to know the boyfriend, he feels better about the relationship. This doesn't seem to be the case here. We don't really know anything about you and your boyfriend, but perhaps the reason your dad won't accept him is that your boyfriend may have shown you some disrespect in the past. Other factors such as age difference may come into play, but we can't say for sure. All we can tell you is that if your dad doesn't accept your boyfriend after getting to know him for two years, maybe there's something he sees though his own life experience that you don't—why not bring the issue up with him one-on-one, and really listen to what he has to say. If he makes a statement you don't agree with, don't get defensive. If you communicate with your dad like an adult, you may be able to reach an adult compromise about your situation—and you may just be able to get him to see things your way.

CG! TIP: Because they've lived longer and had more experiences, sometimes parents do know best. Always at least listen to your parents' opinions when making your own decisions.

GuYs AnD YoUr FaMiLy

Q "My family is moving, which means my boyfriend and I will be miles away from each other. We have a really good relationship, but my parents think we're just kidding ourselves if we think that having a long-distance relationship a good idea. Should we just cut bait?"

A Your parents may have a point, but it might just be that they're trying to protect you from what they feel may be unnecessary pain. A long-distance relationship is a difficult proposition. So many couples who try and make it work just can't. How do you know whether or not it will work for you and your boyfriend? Really think about what it will mean when you two won't be living in the same place anymore. Do you have good phone conversations already? Have you talked about what it will mean when you don't ever get to see someone you want to see all the time? Now, the bright side. With a relationship that's thriving like yours, absence may only make your hearts grow fonder. Just make sure you two discuss challenges and frustrations of they start to come up. Just remember: change can be good. Being apart could be more of a burden than a pleasure to you. So it might be better to take time off while you're apart and the check in when you're back in the same place.

CG! TIP: The only way to truly know if a long-distance relationship will work out is to give it a try.

Q "I've been dating this guy for a few months now and he wants me to meet his parents. He is my first serious boyfriend, and this will be my first time 'meeting the parents.' How can I make a great first impression? Help!"

A What a great, yet nerve-racking experience all in one! You have found someone you really care about, and he is returning the sentiment by asking you to meet his parents. To put your mind at ease a little, if their son adores you, they are more likely to think you're great. Reach out to them—shake hands, make eye contact, and smile—be warm and inviting. But be sure not to be too affectionate towards your boyfriend! Kissing, hugging, and even touching him a lot are inappropriate in front of his parents. Let them know about your hobbies, family, and future plans. Try and keep and even balance between opening up about yourself and letting them respond and talk about themselves and their family—make sure you aren't the only one doing the talking! Offer to lend a hand. If you are eating dinner at their house, volunteer to set the table or clear the dishes. Lastly, send a short thank-you note to say you had a great time. No need to send a gift, just the thought of a quick thank-you is what really counts! The most important thing to do? Remember to be yourself. They'll admire you just as much as your guy does.

CG! TIP: Before you meet your boyfriend's parents, find out about their interests so you can prepare yourself with questions for them.

GuYs AnD YoUr FaMiLy

Q "My boyfriend and I broke up about a month ago, and we might get back together. But my mom and dad have threatened to make my life miserable if we do. Help!"

A The first thing you might want to do is think about why your mom and dad feel so strongly about this. They've let you date before, right? It sounds like they're concerned that your ex is bad news and they want to protect you from getting hurt. What went on with him the first time you were together? Be honest: Is there anything about him they should be worried about? Like, let's say he cheated on you. If so, that's a really good reason not to get back together—and we can totally understand their concern. But if your parents have never liked him for no good reason, then you need to talk to them about it. Make sure that you really understand where they're coming from—and that they understand that you're looking out for yourself, too. It may sound weird, but during the conversation, repeat their points back to them so they know that you get what they're saying. ("Mom, I understand that you think he dresses like a bum.") But then follow up with a good point. ("You've always taught me to value good morals, and Jeff has better morals than anyone I know.") Above all, be sure to stay calm—that'll show your parents how mature (and trustworthy) you are. One last thing: Don't just pretend to hear your parents out. Really listen. Because you never know—they may be right about this guy! Either way, try to always surround yourself with guys who treat you with the love and respect that you deserve.

CG! TIP: Chances are, your parents did their share of dating others before getting married to each other, so believe it or not, they might have some great advice for you!

Q "I'm 16 and my boyfriend is 18. We've been going out for a year and he asked me to go away with him for spring break. I would love to—and I totally trust him—but my parents won't allow it. What should I do?"

A We know this is not what you want to hear, but we totally agree with your parents. Just remember: It isn't so much that they don't trust you or your boyfriend, it's the situation they don't trust. It's really more about you being away from home with your boyfriend and his friends (in other words, no parents), and stuff can happen in those situations—especially if there's drinking, drugs, or partying—even if you're not looking for it. Once you've lived on your own (like college) and showed your parents you can handle all kinds of situations, they'll eventually loosen up. Until then, if you decide to pass on a party because you know people there will be doing drugs or something, tell them. Show them that, yes, you've been soaking up their good morals all these years. In the end, your parents just want you to be safe—can you blame them?

Chapter 7

guys and
your friends

Sure, your best girlfriends are like sisters to you, but do they always have the answers to your guy questions? Sometimes yes, sometimes no. Read on and see what we mean!

GuYs AnD YoUr FrIenDs

Q "I've always been attracted to bad boys, but my friends think I'm just looking to get hurt. I may get my heart broken a lot, but for me, there's nothing hotter than a bad boy. Are my friends right about this?"

A It could be that you're a little wild too, or maybe you just wish you were. But it sounds to us like what your friends are worried about is not that you like the guy with the who-cares-what-they-think attitude, but that you always seem to get burned by these relationships. If you really want to date bad boys, then do so with caution. Take the relationships for the only things that they can ever be—light, casual, and carefree—and yes, exciting. If you believe that you can somehow change this kind of guy, that's when you're going to get hurt. If you're looking for a substantial relationship, then keep your eyes open for the good guys. You never know when one will have just a slight edge of "bad boy," in him and that may be just what you need!

CG! TIP: Don't let the quest for a boyfriend consume you. Instead, have fun with your girlfriends, who always make you feel special.

Q "I've always been really focused on doing well in school, which has meant keeping up a straight-A average and getting involved in lots of extracurricular activities. My friends think that because I always speak up in class that guys may be intimidated by me. I won't pretend to be less smart than guys—does that mean I'm not ready for a relationship?"

A Sounds like you are ready for a relationship—with a guy who totally respects and adores you for those brains and awesome ambition of yours. You have amazing confidence, and no matter what your friends say, that's what really attracts guys—the right kind of guys. As far as your friends go, we think they're just trying to be helpful, but may be a little misguided. Have a talk with them and try to explain your point of view. We hope they come around!

CG! TIP: Never cancel plans with your friends to accept a last-minute date. Not only is this inconsiderate to do to your friends, you'll also send signals to the guy that you're being desperate.

GuYs AnD YoUr FrIenDs

Q **"My friends see relationships with guys as 'us' vs. 'them.' We read somewhere that this is the right approach. But we never get dates. Why?"**

A It's hard not to think of the guy as the enemy when he grunts one-word answers to your questions, or when he says he'll call you and doesn't. But if you think of relationships as "us versus them," then you've set up a situation where you're always playing games, and that means there has to be a winner and a loser. A good relationship doesn't have two opposing sides—it's more like a two-person team where both members are working together to make the relationship great.

Q **"Every time I like a guy, he finds out, even if I'm not obvious about it. Why does this happen?"**

A We hate to tell you this but as much as girlfriends rock, they also talk! If a guy hears he's being gossiped about, it could embarrass him. He'll see you as the cause, and that will kill your chances with him. Keep your feelings secret, and make sure you're the one who controls how he finds out. If things work out, your girls will realize you like him soon enough. Plus, only your diary will know when a guy doesn't like you back, so you'll look like you never get dissed!

Q "My best friend likes the same guy I do. She has some history with him, but when we all hung out, he whispered in my ear that he really likes me, not my best friend, and then he kissed me. Later that night, my friend was upset because she felt I was trying to steal this guy from her. I really like him a lot and want to start something with him, but what's going to happen between my best friend and me?"

A We know you won't want to hear this, but no matter how exciting it feels to have this guy like you, it's not worth jeopardizing your friendship. Here's what you should do with this guy: nothing. We know how much you like him, and we're not saying that the two of you can never be together. But if you really want to keep her friendship, you can't be until your friend is so over him that she'd actually be happy for you. Just remember: If you're meant to be with him, you will be eventually. And if it's not that strong of a connection, it's certainly not worth losing your friend over.

CG! TIP: Your relationships with your girlfriends will probably last longer than your romances. Don't put your friendships in jeopardy for a guy.

GuYs AnD YoUr FrIenDs

Q "I have a really huge crush on my best friend's older brother and I think he really likes me too. Problem is, my friend is really protective over her brother and she'd probably never speak to me again if anything ever happened with me and him. Still, I can't help the way I feel. What should I do?"

A There are a few ways to handle this situation, and we'll start by telling you the worst thing you can do: Dating your friend's brother behind her back. How is it going to feel to hold a secret this big back from her? And how badly will it hurt her when she finds out? Is it really worth it? The ideal thing for you to do is to realize that there are many other guys out there for you to date, and if this one happens to be off-limits for whatever reason, so be it. Of course, if your feelings are so strong that you can't just ignore them, then talk to your friend about it. Tell her how you feel about him, and that you really want to start seeing him. Remember, this girl holds you in high regard as her best friend. If others may not be up to snuff dating her brother, that doesn't mean she feels the same way about you. But if you don't talk to her about it, you'll never know.

CG! TIP: If you like a guy who's off-limits to you, try to decide *before* you go after him if you want him because you really like him, or just because you can't have him.

Q "I really, really liked this guy but I never told my best friend about it and she started going out with him. The problem is, I still like him and he still calls me all the time. What should I do?"

A This guys is not prince charming! Actually, he's more like a toad! You say he's still calling you, which means he was probably calling and leading you on long before he started dating your friend. But now he's involved in a relationship with your best friend and he continues to call you? Not only should you stop taking his calls, you should also come clean to your friend about what's been going on. It's not fair to her to let her keep dating a guy you know is a jerk. Chances are slim that she may think you're making things up because she never knew you liked him. In fact, it's more like she'll be a little hurt that you didn't confide in her in the first place. But, she'll probably be more concerned that the guy she's seeing is playing you both and then put his sorry butt on her list of exes!

GuYs AnD YoUr FrIenDs

Q "I kissed a guy who has a girlfriend and now my best friend is mad at me. I don't think she has a right to be, and it really hurts that she's judging me. To her, what I did was stupid. To me, it was what felt right at the time.... Shouldn't she support me because she's my friend? How can I talk to her about this?"

A Your friend is bugging out because true friendships are based on having things in common like values and beliefs. Because of the kissing episode, she's probably feeling that you have different values than her, and is upset about it. The only way to figure out how to deal with your friend is to ask yourself this: How do you feel about what happened between you and the guy? Is there a part of you that thinks you messed up, yet still doesn't want to be judged by her? Then tell her you totally hear her and agree with her point. And that life is all about learning from mistakes. That should smooth things over. If it doesn't, you've done the best you can, and she needs time to chill out. But if you feel like you did absolutely nothing wrong by kissing that guy, it might be a sign that you and your friend are growing apart. As we get older, people's values and beliefs can change. You may end up clashing with certain people around you—that could be the case here. But your first step to solving this is to figure out how you feel about what you did. Then take it from there.

Q "Recently, a good friend of mine set me up on a blind date, but when I arrived, and saw him from far away, I thought the guy was ugly. I hate to admit this, but I just bolted. Why would my friend set me up with such an unattractive guy? Do you think it means she thinks that I'm unattractive?"

A Everyone's had the experience of being set up on a blind date with someone they have had nothing in common with and absolutely no attraction to, and thought the same thing you're thinking right now. But guess what? Our friends hold us in highest regard, which is what makes them our friends. Of course, just because you're friends with someone doesn't mean you're going to have the same tastes as them. Chances are, your friend thought this was a nice guy who she probably thought was cute and that you'd hit it off with him. By standing this guy up, you not only made your friend look bad, but you also unnecessarily hurt someone else's feelings—his. Sometimes you have to give people a chance. Just because he didn't look like Adam Brody when you saw him doesn't mean you should have walked out on him. Who knows—he may have kept you laughing all night with his hilarious wit and humor. And even if a romance never blossomed, you may have missed out on making a really good friend.

ChApTeR 8

are you really ready?

Yeah, he's ready. He's told you he's ready. A lot! But
you're not sure if you are. So what should you do?
Read other CosmoGIRL!s questions on the same topic
and see if any of them sound like your situation....
We hope our advice will help you make the right
decision for your body and your heart!

ArE YoU ReAlLy rEady?

Q "I've been going out with my boyfriend for three months, and all we've really done so far is make out. A lot of my friends have already gone all the way, but I'm not ready yet. I'm afraid I'm going to lose him soon if I don't have sex with him. What should I do?"

A Don't let the thought that you may lose him push you into going further than you actually want to. Remember: A girl who doesn't reveal everything to a guy all at once will stay more interesting to him. Which brings us to the question of why are you afraid you're going to lose him. From what you tell us, he hasn't brought up the subject of going all the way, so it may be possible that he's comfortable with the pace you've been moving at as much as you. Don't worry about what everyone else is doing. When it comes right down to it, the issue of sex is between you and him. When he's ready, he'll bring it up. And if you're not ready yet, he'll have to wait until you are. If he's not willing to do that and breaks up with you, you'll know he didn't really deserve to be with you—and make yourself available to find someone who does.

CG! TIP: If you decide to have sex, be sure you're doing it because you're ready—and not because you're feeling pressured.

Q "I've been with my boyfriend for two months and it seems we never go anywhere on a date except my room, his room, or the back seat of his car. I've tried to suggest we do more than just hook up, but he doesn't seem to be interested in anything else. Is he using me for sex?"

A That's a hard question to address without actually knowing your boyfriend or very much about your relationship, but if you're asking it, we hate to tell you that you probably already know what the answer is. Want to know for sure? Think about what really goes on between you two—and be honest with yourself. Do you wish he'd be more attentive when you're together rather than just being interested in getting physical? If you've told him that you'd like to do more than just hook up and he doesn't agree, it seems like he's only in this for the action—and you deserve much more than that.

CG! TIP: Listen to your gut. If you feel like things are moving too fast, they probably are.

Are YoU ReAlLy ready?

Q "I've had sex with this guy I like four times, but he still hasn't asked me out. He's had a girlfriend on and off while having sex with me. What do you think I should do?"

A You can start by not having sex with him again. This guy obviously doesn't get how amazing you are. If he did, he would treat you better. That said, don't fixate on what you can do to change him. His bad behavior is pretty much a red flag that should be telling you "Loser alert! Keep moving." But sometimes it's hard to read guys' signals right. We see an obvious sign, but instead of reading "Keep away," we read "Fix me." Here's an important piece of advice: Don't get involved with someone until you're sure he values you enough to keep things exclusive. When you hook up with him too early, you're giving him the message that you don't value yourself—which isn't the case. If you respect yourself, guys will follow your lead.

> **CG! TIP:** Some guys will say anything to speed things up when it comes to sex. Be aware of how you're truly feeling, not just what he's saying in the moment.

Q "My boyfriend and I just started having sex a few months ago, and even though I know he cares about me, I feel frustrated and used for days after, each time. What's wrong with me?"

A There's nothing wrong with you. But we're guessing that you probably feel guilty about having sex. Maybe someone you respect (like a parent or friend) wouldn't approve of what you and your boyfriend are doing. Only you would know the answer to that. Sex is supposed to be special, safe, and enjoyable—and if you're feeling guilty, you're probably not enjoying it. Or, maybe the reality of sex isn't what you expected it to be. A lot of girls have a mental picture that sex is this romantic experience with background music and great lighting. Sometimes it is, but often, especially in the beginning, it's not. No matter why you feel used, though, if something bothers you, stop doing it and talk to your boyfriend. Spell out your feelings; he won't know what's going on with you unless you tell him. This means saying that you need more talking, eye contact, kissing, whatever, to connect more OR that you need to cool things down for a while. The point is, you have to feel respected and comfortable, and that will take work—from both of you.

CG! TIP: Want to get intimate without getting too close? Draw pictures of one other and label each of your favorite parts of the other.

ArE YoU ReAlLY rEadY?

Q "I got drunk at a party and slept with a lot of guys. I didn't get pregnant, but I did get a bad reputation. Now people look at me funny in the halls at school. What should I do?"

A We can't sugarcoat this one for you: You've put yourself in a situation that's not easy to fix. But knowing that upfront will help you—if you can keep up your strength, you will rise above this. Now, before we go any further: If you haven't already gone to the gynecologist, go and get tested for STDs to be sure you've got a clean bill of health. As for cleaning up your rep? Well, think about what politicians do when they get into hot water: They address rumors head-on. So when you're out, avoid alcohol altogether to send the message that you do have self-control. And if people ask you why you're not drinking, say something like "Drinking's gotten me into trouble in the past" to let people know you're not afraid to admit your mistake and move on. Doing this takes fuel from the fire—it's no fun to talk about someone who doesn't seem to care. Also, become known for something you can be proud of. Whether it's producing the best charity dance ever or becoming a champion athlete, redefine yourself according to who you know you are. It will take time before people let you live this one down. But keep your head high and be committed to living a life you can be proud of. That's what matters.

CG! TIP: As tempting as a hot hookup session may be, step back before lust takes over and ask yourself if the emotional risk is worth the physical reward.

Q "How come guys are the only ones who get horny? And how come they always want oral sex?"

A Girls can be just as into sex as guys are. The difference is that our society teaches guys that it's "macho," and therefore okay, to talk about sex or make lewd comments in public. Girls tend to keep their thoughts private because, unfair as it is, a girl who talks about sex may be seen as "slutty." As for oral sex, guys like it because it feels similar to intercourse (the tissue inside the mouth feels like the inside of the vagina), and they consider it "safer" because you can't get pregnant. But since you can get STDs from oral sex, it's essential that you use condoms to protect yourself if you even decide to go through with it, which you don't—repeat—*don't* have to. As you know, the only truly safe option is not having sex at all.

CG! TIP: You don't owe a guy anything, especially not sex. Show him you respect yourself and he'll respect you too.

"You Should
be in
My Space:
You Should
be in
My Life.":

serious guy issues

Sometimes the stuff that goes on with guys is a little too weighty for us to carry around on our own. But remember: That's what your parents, other adults you can trust, and CosmoGIRL! are there for! So if any of these scenarios sound familiar, be sure to get help. We care too much about you for you not to!

SeRIoUS GuY ISsuEs

Q "I'm 18 years old and my boyfriend is 13 years older than me. He wants to start a family, which I think is sweet, but it's scary. He's the only guy I've ever dated, and I don't want to do anything I'll regret later. How can I tell him I'm not ready to start a family without him breaking up with me?"

A Okay, the first thing that's making us really nervous about this situation is the age difference. We're sorry to have to tell you this, but we think you already know: This guy's much too old for you. At this time in your life, it's time to start thinking about who your adult self is and what you want to do with your future. Want to go away to college? That's going to be pretty difficult with young children! The problem is that you are both in different stages in your life. He's experienced life as an adult; he's ready to settle down. You still have a lot of living and learning to do. If we were you, we wouldn't be afraid of him breaking up with you if you told him you didn't want to start a family at this point in your life. We hate to say it, but if he did, it might be the best thing for both of you right now.

CG! TIP: Be careful about dating much older guys. You may have very different goals for the relationship, which can cause you to get hurt.

Q "I've got an obsession with somebody. The thing is, he's famous. But I'm not just a fanatic—I'm in love with him and was even before he got so big. I'm sure no girl feels the same way for him as I do! I'm going crazy because I can't have him. What should I do?"

A We've all been into celebrities, so we know how you feel about your famous crush. But what you need to know is that as intense as your feelings may be they're not feelings of real love. Not to be harsh, but let's face it: You don't even *know* him personally! And the biggest problem with obsessing over a celebrity is that it could keep you from forming real-life relationships. So what you need to do is get back to the things you loved to do before your obsession began. Because when you're not busy, it's easy to drift into Celeb Land. But when you're doing stuff you like, you'll be too distracted to obsess. You don't have to forget your crush, just become a true supporter of his art—buy his CDs, go to his concerts, that kind of thing—instead. By shifting your energy away from him and back to yourself, you'll experience life—and be open to finding a guy who's accessible and who'll be able to love you back the way you deserve.

CG! TIP: Having crushes is healthy, but try not to give your heart away to someone who won't reciprocate your feelings.

SeRIoUS GuY ISsuEs

Q "I think I have a crush on my friend's dad! I find myself flirting with him and he flirts back! He jokes around saying that we're going to run away together, and when he hugs me, it's not an ordinary hug. I've had sexual feeling about him, and I want to tell him, but I need a second opinion before I do."

A We think you should get away from this situation as soon as you can. For so many reasons, you're heading for trouble here. For one, getting involved in a sexual relationship with your friend's father could play on your mind in bigger ways than you can realize right now. It could have a bad effect on your future relationships. And think about how it will affect your relationship with your friend when she finds out you've been seeing her dad! On top of that, this man should not be flirting with you. For one, it would be absolutely illegal for him to be involved with you if you are a minor. Even if you aren't, by acting on sexual impulses with you, he is completely disrespecting his daughter and his family. Is this really the kind of guy you want to be involved with on any level? Our advice: Stop going to your friend's house and avoid this man at whatever cost. No good could ever come from this situation!

CG! TIP: If an older guy starts making advances on you, tell an adult you trust right away.

Q "I'm in love with my boyfriend, but I'm always hitting him. Sometimes I'm just being playful, but last night I hit him really hard—and I knew it hurt because he got really angry. I regretted it right away. I've always been afraid of being hit by a boyfriend. But I'm the one who's doing the hitting, even though I know my guy would never lay a hand on me. I think I need some help."

A You're right—you do need help with this. Being in this type of relationship is not only bad for your boyfriend, it's bad for *you* too. We obviously don't know much about you and we don't want to guess. But we wonder what your parents were like to each other and to you. Was there any violence or abuse—even if it was verbal? Were you abused by anyone in the past? Sometimes people who were mistreated as children get so used to being surrounded by abuse that they continue to create abusive situations for themselves in their relationships. This is the kind of thing you should talk to a counselor about, because it's the first step to getting a handle on why you've been hitting him. Do you feel comfortable talking to your parents or a counselor at school? If not, try calling Childhelp USA at 800-422-4453. You should start taking steps now to understand where your anger is rooted so you can start paying attention to the cause of it, and start treating the symptom (hitting) at the same time. For now, we think you should cool it with your boyfriend. We're not saying break up with him, but give yourselves some time to digest what you've been going through and come up with a game plan to start getting help. Take the time and make that phone call. Those first steps are the hardest to take because they depend on you openly talking about a tough subject. But do it. You owe it to yourself to resolve what's going on inside you. Because if you let a problem like this continue, you could end up losing people in your life who you really love.

CG! TIP: Any time you feel yourself getting out of control is a good time to get help!

Q "I haven't dated a lot, but recently, I started hanging out with my brother's friend. We spent two nights together, and I thought things were going well, until he told me that he still loves his ex. I find myself wanting to see him, so I go to our friends' houses hoping to run into him. Is this normal, or am I psycho?"

A It's so hard when you still have feelings for someone who at one point was really nice to you, because you hold out hope that he'll be that way again. But from what you've said, it seems like this guy is not interested in you romantically. The longer you build your schedule around this guy, the longer you'll keep pining for him, and the harder it will be to get over him. We wish we could say something to make these feelings go away, but we can't. You have to force yourself to move on. When you find yourself thinking that you should call your friend because this guy might be over there, stop and do something just for you. Call another friend who's completely unconnected to him, or write in your journal. You've got an enormous ability to open yourself up to love—and that'll be so amazing when you meet the guy who's right for you.

CG! TIP: Live your life for you. Don't plan your life around any guy!

SeRIoUS GuY ISsuEs

Q "I'm new to my town, and let's just say I've gotten with a group of guys and I wish I could take it back—but I can't. So basically, I'm known as a slut in school. Girls hate me, and guys are skeptical of me. I don't want to be looked down upon because I hooked up with guys. How can I get over this label?"

A Let's focus less on what people are saying about you and more on why you were with those guys. Did you hook up with them because you're new and you wanted to fit in? Sometimes, girls have a tendency to want to get over their feelings of loneliness or sense of not belonging by getting physical with the guys. It feels like the quickest and most intense way to feel connected to someone. But unfortunately, it's never a real or lasting connection. You can't change what you've already done or what people are saying about you right now (don't even try—you'll just get upset and frustrated). What you do have control over is everything you do from this moment on. Hold off on getting physical with anyone. Spend the rest of your school year getting to know your classmates as people—the girls and the guys. Strike up a conversation with anyone you think you can relate to (talk about the things you have in common, like a class). And remember, don't just talk to the guys—meet girls too. What you need right now are friends and allies. It does take longer to build relationships this way, but you'll be building ones with solid foundations. With friendships like that, you'll feel more secure because you'll know that people like you for you. And little by little, you'll find that everyone will know that you're a lot more than just a label. But in order for them to realize that, you need to show them all those amazing sides of you that they never knew were there!

Q "I've been going out with my boyfriend for more than five years. I really love him, don't get me wrong, but lately I find myself having really strong feelings for his sister. I'm so confused. I always thought I was straight, but now I'm not so sure. Could I be gay or bisexual? I don't know what to do. Please help!"

A It's normal in adolescence to question your sexuality, but that doesn't necessarily mean you are gay or even bisexual—you might just be curious about that world. However, if you feel this is more than just a passing curiosity, and that you do find women sexually attractive, you may want to discuss the situation with a counselor who can help you work through and become comfortable with your feelings. If you are scared to speak to someone you know, or if confusion about your sexuality is making you depressed or even suicidal, you can always call the Girls and Boys Town National Hotline at 800-448-3000 for guidance.

CG! TIP: Having feelings for a person of the same sex as you does not necessarily mean you're gay. Talk your feelings over with an adult you trust.

SERIOUS GUY ISSUES

Q "I've been dating my guy for six months. When we met I was straight, but now I'm bisexual. What will happen if I tell him?"

A You should tell him, but when you do, move slowly and wisely. Make sure you do it at a time when he's prepared to listen to you carefully. It's important to be honest with people, no matter how hard it can be. Be prepared for his reaction: While he might be cool about it at first, he may be angry about it later on. Your admission may even cause him to question his own sexuality or his "manliness." In other words, if he's such a good boyfriend, why is his girlfriend all of a sudden interested in women? Whether he has or hasn't been a great boyfriend has nothing to do with what's happening to you, but it will be hard for him not to take it personally. Make sure he know that, and prepare yourself for what the outcome may be. Staying together may prove to be too difficult for the both of you.

Q "I'm caught in a love triangle with my long-term boyfriend and a new guy. I'm tired of hiding and sneaking around, but I love them both—and I can't choose between them. I just want to be with one person. What should I do?"

A Honestly, you should stop dating both of them. Right now in your situation, no one's getting a fair shake. Your long-term boyfriend is being cheated on, and your new guy is in a sticky situation. He may be someone you really like, or he may just be the bridge you're using to get over the pain of cutting off a long-term connection. This can't be fair to either of these guys, and more importantly, it can't be fair to yourself. If you want to figure out what you have to do, you need to take yourself out of the situation. It may be that you want one of these guys more than the other—and it also might turn out that you don't want to be with either. But all you're doing now is setting up a disastrous situation in which the only outcome is three people getting very hurt.

CG! TIP: Being honest in relationships is the only way you can be true to yourself.

SeRIoUS GuY ISsuEs

Q "Last year, when I was 13, I skipped school one day to hang out with one of my brother's friends, who I'd always had a big crush on. We were supposed to hang out with his girlfriend, too, but for some reason, she never showed. Soon, he started to put the moves on me, but I resisted because he had a girlfriend and I had a boyfriend at the time. And then he raped me. I screamed and kicked and tried to get away but nothing helped. I still haven't been able to get over the emotional pain of what happened. What should I do?"

A It's awful what happened to you. But please know that you can't possibly handle something this big by yourself—no one could. You'll want to start by talking to an adult you can trust, like your mother or a counselor. If you're scared to talk to someone you know, you can get confidential help by calling RAINN'S (Rape, Abuse & Incest National Network) toll-free hotline at 800-656-HOPE. They can give you direction, including helping you find a professional you can speak to on a regular basis to help yourself start healing.

Q "My friend woke up in a strange place one morning after a party. She didn't know what happened—she was too drunk to remember even though she didn't drink that much. Anyway, when she opened her eyes, she was half dressed and she has a feeling that she may have been raped. Now the rest of my friends and I are scared to go to parties because we're terrified the same thing will happen to us. What should we do?"

A You don't have to say good-bye to your social life. What happened to your friend does not happen at every party, but we will tell you that you guys should look out for each other from now on. If she hasn't already, your friend needs to get herself checked out at a clinic. She needs to bring any evidence—like hair or stained clothes—with her. And if possible, she should not shower or brush her teeth before she goes. In the future, when you go to a party or a club, pair with a friend and check in through the night. Whatever you do, don't leave without each other. The best way to stay in control at a club or party is not to drink at all. The number one date rape drug, after all, is alcohol itself. But if you do drink, always get your own drinks (including non-alcoholic ones) and never leave them unattended.

Q "I never told anyone this, but my boyfriend has a very violent temper. He's never hit me, but he gets so angry, I'm afraid he will. Do you think I'm over-reacting? What should I do?"

A It breaks our hearts to say this but you're not alone. One out of every five teenage girls experience dating violence, and noticing these behaviors early is the key to protecting yourself. That means seeing the pattern before anything drastic happens. Relationship violence rarely flares out of nowhere. Most of the time, a boyfriend who hits is a particular type of guy: He showers you with attention when he's in a good mood but gets incredibly jealous of other people in your life, like friends and guys. He's possessive, always wanting to know what you do and who you do it with. If he doesn't get his way, he'll lose his temper—and then apologize as soon as he calms down. A violent guy also acts explosively towards others, like his mother or random people. Don't think he won't act the same way toward you. Do you find yourself making excuses to friends or family for the way he acts? Have you started changing the way you look or whom you hang out with solely to please him? Sometimes boyfriends might suggest you do your hair a certain way, but we don't mean once in a while—we mean a recurring pattern. Guys who repeatedly disrespect you and your friends and family or who constantly try to change you aren't okay—they fit the "violent" profile. Violence often escalates after a breakup so make everyone you know, including your parents and school counselors, aware that you're about to end it. If your school doesn't help, contact a local domestic violence group for advice on breaking up safely. Find one through the National Domestic Violence Hotline at 800-799-SAFE.

CG! TIP: If a guy loses his temper quickly or gets into a lot of fights, he might be prone to violence. Think twice about getting involved with guys like this.

InDeX

InDeX